W9-BHR-365

the
button
book

the button book

BY DIANA EPSTEIN

RUNNING PRESS

PHILADELPHIA · LONDON

Library of Congress Cataloging-in-Publication Number
96-67142
ISBN 1-56138-739-8

This book may be ordered by mail from the publisher.
Please include $1.00 for postage and handling.
But try your bookstore first!

Running Press Book Publishers
125 South Twenty-second Street
Philadelphia, Pennsylvania 19103-4399

Contents

Introduction

The button. How is it that such a mundane object can be so important in our daily lives? From our first baby sleepers to the threadbare cardigan sweaters of our twilight years, buttons are constantly with us, securing and adorning our every garment. Yet, most of us give little thought to them—except perhaps when one is missing.

But buttons are filled with nostalgia. As children we adored their various shapes, sizes, colors, and textures. Learning how to button was one of our earliest lessons. And buttons were a part of our favorite games—remember Who's Got the Button? We've used them for tops, whistles, and the eyes and noses of handmade sock puppets. They were our family treasures and heirlooms, stored in special tins that were brought out on rainy days, or when mother was sewing.

But for some, buttons remain sources of endless intrigue and fascination, objects to be pursued and hoarded, like gems or gold. And it's no small wonder. Buttons have a long and elegant history, and their value as art, as well as artifact, is ever-increasing. The study of buttons includes a survey of every imaginable natural and man-made material. Buttons reflect every kind of art and craft known, and they record every phase of our social history, from our primitive past to our streamlined present.

Discover the wonderment of buttons and the sense of passion they inspire through the quotes, trivia, anecdotes, folklore, and colorful photos complied here, in a little book that's, well . . . as cute as a button.

20TH-CENTURY, ASIAN
PASSEMENTERIE BUTTON

button
your lip

BUTTONS IN QUOTES
AND LANGUAGE

The word button
is derived from the
French *bouton,*
meaning anything
round—a bud, knob,
or protuberance.
Interestingly, button
wasn't used as a verb
in English until the
thirteenth century.

19TH-CENTURY FRENCH, BRASS
AND VELVET PERFUME BUTTON

12

Denis Diderot, the eighteenth-century French encyclopedist, devoted eight pages to buttons and buttonmakers.

Buttons are the fossils of the sartorial world, enduring long past the garments they were designed to hold together.

Martha Stewart
20th-century lifestyle expert,
writer, and publisher

In 1844, James Harper was elected mayor of New York. That year he set up the first uniformed police force for New York City. These uniforms had large copper buttons—hence these civil servants came to be known as *Cops* or *Coppers*.

Button man is an American slang expression for a rank and file member of the Mafia.

Between 1840–1950, hotel bellboys
and pages were commonly referred
to as *Buttons,* no doubt for the
many buttons on their uniforms.

I still connect buttons and beads with greed. When I run my hands through piles of them, it might as well be piles of money. . . . Buttons and beads are like fetishes —very powerful symbols with many dimensions, full of memories and meaning, all very subjective and personal to each person.

Sally Stang
20th-century glass
beadmaker

One can never have
too many buttons.

Laurella Lederer
20th-century button
collector and dealer

19TH-CENTURY PAINTING
ON IVORY UNDER GLASS,
PROBABLY FRENCH

Buttons are and were a work of art. They told the world where you were in society.

Sonni Helmer
20th-century button
jewelry designer

Once in the dress she studied it
in the mirror and decided she had
forgotten how unbecoming it was,
but she was too weary to march
her fingers down the long row of
buttons again.

Irene Cleaton
20th-century
mystery writer

Biographies are but the clothes
and buttons of the man—
the biography of the man himself
cannot be written.

Mark Twain (1835–1910)
American writer
and humorist

As a man is judged
by the company he keeps,
so a garment is judged by
the buttons you find on it.

Anonymous

Buttons have been
used in the game of
checkers, in various
forms of hopscotch,
and to count off
"He loves me,
he loves me not."

Button, Button, Who's Got the Button? is the jingle that accompanies a classic counting game taught to kindergartners.

20TH-CENTURY AMERICAN BAKELITE, CIRCA 1935

You can have
the shirt off my back—
but you can't have the buttons.

Nancy Bartholomew Fink
20th-century button collector
and president of the
National Button Society

I've collected buttons for over thirty-five years and have never stopped learning from them. My current favorites are golf buttons . . . I'm still searching for "a hole in one."

Lois Pool
20th-century button collector
and secretary of the
National Button Society

More can be learned
about a country and
its people and culture
from their buttons than
can be learned from
all their coins and
stamps put together.

Susan G. Porter
20th-century
button collector

19TH-CENTURY
JAPANESE SATSUMA
PORCELAIN

31

Collecting buttons has increased
my vocabulary and . . . created a
passion for subjects—from Snoopy
to Joan of Arc.

Bill Stone
20th-century
button collector

There are obvious reasons why button collecting appeals to so many people. These tiny antiques are portable and, when compared to furniture or paintings of the same vintage, very affordable. Many are extraordinarily beautiful works of art in themselves. And buttons pack a lot of social history into a very small package.

Diana Epstein
20th-century button expert,
collector, and writer

What I love about buttons is that each one is like a tiny, evocative event. They celebrate historical incidents, serve as a microcosm of the culture from which they arise, and reflect the aesthetic sensibilities of their time.

Millicent Safro
20th-century button expert,
collector, and writer

I am forever changing the buttons
on my clothes, usually for the same
reason that I correct a drawing or
shift colors around in my paintings:
it sharpens the total effect and
creates harmony.

Jim Dine
20th-century artist

There's surely something
charming in seeing the smallest
thing done so thoroughly,
as if to remind the careless,
that whatever is worth doing is
worth doing well.

Charles Dickens
(1812–1870)
English novelist

If a garment is logical,
it will not have buttons
or pockets merely for
ornament. Buttons will
button and pockets will
be designed to hold
things conveniently.

Monsieur Poiret
20th-century
Parisian dressmaker

Forget about buttoning up your overcoat—beautiful buttons should be framed and hung on the wall.

*Mario Buatta
20th-century interior decorator
and lecturer*

Said Tim unto those jurymen,
  You need not waste your breath,
For I confess myself at once
  The author of her death.
And oh!—when I reflect upon
  The blood that I have spilt,
Just like a button is my soul,
  Inscribed with double guilt!

Thomas Hood (1799–1845)
English poet

EARLY 20TH-CENTURY
ENGLISH ART NOUVEAU
SILVER, HALLMARKED

I had a soul above buttons.

George Colman the Younger
(1762–1836)
English Dramatist

Look, Darling!
Those *buttons!* To *die!*

Françoise de la Renta
(Wife of 20th-century fashion
designer, Oscar de la Renta)

In the first few years of my collecting, I often heard my husband ask, "How is it you can sit up to 2 A.M. in your button room every night sewing buttons on cards, and I can't get one on my shirts?"

Sally Luscomb
20th-century button expert,
writer, and lecturer

When pressed,
there's nothing like a button.

Elsa Klensch
Television news personality
and writer

On Fortune's Cap,
we are not the very button.

William Shakespeare
(1564–1616)
English dramatist and poet

- The term *brass buttons* suggests authority and service.

- When we *buttonhole* a person, we arrest his attention.

- A *buttoned-down* person, group, or occasion would be extremely conservative.

Button-related Expressions:

- *Not worth a button* means to lack any value.

- *On the button* means to be on target. In the context of boxing, it refers to the point of the chin.

- When someone must be *taken down a buttonhole,* he's too clever for his own good.

- When we say, *button up your*

overcoat, we are conveying
warmth and concern.

- **Dash my button!** is an
  old-fashioned expletive.

- If you are told to **button your lip**,
  keep your mouth closed.

- If you are **bursting your buttons**,
  you must be very prideful.

- If you have **lost your buttons**,
  your judgment (or sanity) may
  be in question.

During the Civil War,
certain regiments of infantry wore
large globular brass buttons.
One day, a wag named these
soldiers *Dough Boys* because their
buttons reminded him of a boiled
dumpling often served to the army.
The nickname soon caught on.

To me, uniform buttons are more truly fascinating than any other kind. They are the buttons that have seen the world, and have had their own part in its history.

Dorothy Foster Brown
20th-century button expert,
artist, and author

There is an island in
Hingham, Massachusetts
called Button Island.
This is the only island
in the world named for
a button.

19TH-CENTURY FRENCH BRASS AND
CUT-STEEL PICTURE BUTTON

Button is actually a proper name, though not a very popular one in America. One of the most famous bearers of it was Button Gwinnet, a signer of the Declaration of Independence. He was born is Glouchester, England in 1735.

simply

a fastenating

BUTTON TRIVIA

Eighteenth-century aristocrat
Louis XV once had a set of
buttons, each of which
functioned as a working watch.

Louis XV reportedly had his own *boutonnier* to assure the splendor and perfection of his buttons.

19TH-CENTURY
FRENCH ENAMEL
AND CUT-STEEL

George Washington was apparently adverse to all marks of distinction. Yet, on one 4th of July, he received the Society of the Cincinnati wearing a regimental uniform that had buttons with the image of an eagle, richly set with diamonds.

The Hayden & Scovill Company once made a set of solid gold buttons bearing General George Washington's profile. They were presented to General LaFayette during his visit to America in 1824, as a specimen of American skill in die-cutting.

EARLY 19TH-CENTURY
AMERICAN GILT

The first buttons made in the United States were made of metal. In 1750, Caspar Wistar, a German immigrant, began manufacturing brass buttons in Philadelphia.

According to legend, a duel between Andrew Jackson, the seventh president of the United States, and Charles Dickinson, took place in Tennessee. Both were good shots although Dickinson was purported to be better. The night before the duel, Jackson's best friend, Overton, advised him to wear a particular coat having large, heavy silver buttons. The next morning, Dickinson aimed at the button over Jackson's heart and fired. Jackson fired back, killing his opponent. Jackson suffered only some broken bones and bruises to his chest from the impact of Dickinson's bullet against the heavy silver button. Fortunately for Jackson, the night before, Overton had moved the very button that protected him.

The earliest known buttons are from about 2,000 B.C. Excavations in Egypt unearthed several examples of button shapes, but no there was no evidence that they'd been used to fasten garments. These buttons were probably ornamental rather than utilitarian.

PREHISTORIC
STONE BUTTONS

Crusaders brought the button to Europe from the Middle East. Buttons made closer-fitting garments possible; dressmakers and tailors began making long, tightly buttoned sleeves for women's and men's garments that buttoned from chin to waist.

According to fashion historians, the reason men's shirt buttons are on the right dates back the fifteenth century. Men generally dressed themselves. Because it's easier for most people to button their clothes from right to left, the button was placed on the right side.

Women's clothes have buttons on the left because those who could afford the expensive buttons during the fifteenth century had dressing servants. These maids, being predominantly right-handed and having to fasten their mistresses' garments while facing the buttons head-on, found this task easier if the buttons were placed on the left side. Tailors complied and the convention has never been altered since.

The Chinese used to wear five buttons on their coat fronts as symbols of the five principal virtues: Humanity, Justice, Order, Prudence, and Rectitude.

The Amish consider buttons too ornamental, and they associate them with the military. To ensure simplicity of dress, they have traditionally used metal hooks and eyes (or pins) in place of buttons.

In the film *The Cocoanuts* (1929), Harpo Marx ate the buttons off a bellman's vest. The gag was made possible by licorice buttons.

Charles De Gaulle
collected buttons
from French army
uniforms.

Jacqueline Kennedy Onassis
collected rare French
enamel buttons.

According to some button historians, Napoleon Bonaparte is credited with instituting metal buttons on military coat sleeves. By having buttons sewn around the cuffs of his soldiers' sleeves, he was trying to break them of the habit of wiping their noses on them. According to others, it was Queen Elizabeth I of England who was responsible for this fashion vestige.

The convention of having buttons on the lower sleeves of a man's sports coat or suit jacket are symbolic of a time when these buttons actually opened and turned back to reveal the fine, lace-trimmed linen shirt sleeves of wealthy men.

In the 1800s, the head of a London charity whose members were known as Pearlies, had the idea of decorating his trousers with a double row of mother-of-pearl buttons. This caught on, and soon other members of the association began sewing buttons on their clothes. By the nineties, mother-of-pearl-button madness was in full swing. In fact, after one zealous member of the charity covered a complete set of tails with mother-of-pearl buttons, a Pearly King and Pearly Queen began appearing at all the fetes of the association with their clothes wholly covered in buttons. This required twenty to thirty thousand buttons for a man's suit and as many as sixty thousand for a woman's evening dress.

In the 1940s, one Kansas button enthusiast reportedly sewed more than 6,000 buttons on a muslin cape. She used 900 yards of thread to mount the buttons.

Between 1860–1900, young American girls voraciously collected beautiful buttons on long strings, known as charm or love strings. The goal was to collect 999, and then the string's owner would see her future husband.

English boys carried on a lively trade in buttons, as well. They attached specific values and names to various types of buttons, and strictly adhered to this accepted form

of exchange. "Sinkeys,"
concave metal buttons with holes
for sewing, were "one-ers."
"Shankeys," were either "two-ers"
or "three-ers," depending on size,
beauty, or uniqueness. "Liveries"
were metal buttons from the uniforms of servants and were rated as
"three-ers," "four-ers," or "five-ers."
"Six-ers" were bronze buttons bearing images of animals, or symbols
of various sports.

Much of the story and history of buttons lies buried in old documents—wills, diaries, letters, inventories, bills, and newspaper accounts of the costumes worn by royalty or other prominent people.

In George III's will, he left forty coat buttons valued at £4,000 and twenty-six waistcoat buttons valued at £1,000.

As a bridal gift,
Louis XIV gave to
Mlle. d'Abigne,
sixteen sleeve buttons
valued at 12,000 francs.

19TH-CENTURY FRENCH
PAINTING ON IVORY

In South Kingston, Rhode Island, historian William Babcock Weeden found the following description in a planter's estate inventory: "Stephen Hazard's best suit was adorned with silver buttons and he wore a beaver hat."

The richest looking and most elaborate buttons were made during the 1700s. They were intended to be worn by men.

In 17th-century Connecticut, anyone who wore gold or silver buttons was taxed.

19TH-CENTURY FRENCH
ENAMEL AND CUT-STEEL

During the Renaissance,
masks were an essential part
of a lady's wardrobe.
Some masks fastened behind
the ears. One type, however,
was held in place with two
buttons, which the wearer placed
in the corners of her mouth.

In 1290, Queen Elinor, wife of Edward I of England, attended her sister's wedding in a dress that had been renovated for the occasion. This gown was trimmed with 636 silver buttons.

In 1520, King Francis I of France ordered 13,400 buttons from his jeweler. The buttons were sewn onto a black velveteen suit, which Francis wore to a meeting with Henry VII of England. The suit was no doubt created to impress the English king; Francis was seeking a political alliance with his northern neighbor.

In World War I the British Army used 367 different kinds of buttons. Buttons were considered so important to front-line troops that any kind of a button could be requisitioned and delivered within eight hours. The British Army spent $500,000 per year just for the paste used to polish buttons.

Louis XIV had a great weakness for buttons. During his lifetime he spent $6,000,000 on buttons; $600,000 in one year alone.

18TH-CENTURY FRENCH
PAINTING ON IVORY

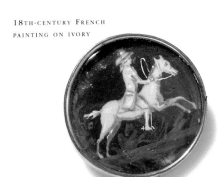

Some consider it bad luck
to wear shirts with buttons.
Duke Ellington insisted on
pullover shirts for that reason.
He was so superstitious, in
fact, that he once delayed a
concert for thirty-five minutes
while assistants searched
for a shirt with no buttons.

19TH-CENTURY
SCOTTISH KILT BUTTONS

Long ago, Scottish warriors wore heavy, diamond-shaped silver buttons on their kilts to assure them of a proper burial if they were killed on foreign soil. The value of the buttons was such that it covered the cost involved. Diamond-shaped silver buttons still appear on Highland dress, though for decorative purposes only.

The collar on English-style polo shirts buttons down. This feature prevents any flapping when the polo player's horse gallops.

SHIRT - BUTTONS

PEARL
SHIRT
BUTTONS

The two buttons on the back of a man's long-tailed coat were originally used for fastening back the tails of his coat when riding horseback.

20TH-CENTURY AMERICAN PEARL BUTTONS ON DISPLAY CARDS

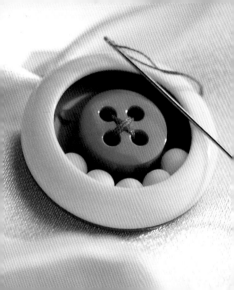

cute as a
button

BUTTON DESIGN

Common subjects on Victorian metal picture buttons include animals, architecture, astronomy, children, the circus, coins, cupids, fables, fops, history, land and water scenes, modes of transportation, music, mythology, oriental design, pastimes, people, plants, religion, stories, symbols, theatrical motifs, and zodiac signs.

Perfumery buttons, popular in Victorian times, contained cotton or wool swatches that were moistened with scent.

19TH-CENTURY
BRASS AND VELVET
FRENCH PERFUME

Black glass (or Jet) buttons were made popular by Queen Victoria, who wore them to mourn the death of her husband, Prince Albert.

Memorial (or hair) buttons originated in the late 1700s. Usually the initials of the departed were woven into a monogram of fine gold wire and laid against a background of crimson silk or braided hair. This was covered by a thick crystal that was set in gold. Sometimes a gold skull and cross bones was added.

19TH-CENTURY BLACK GLASS, PROBABLY CZECHOSLOVAKIAN

Benvenuto Cellini (1500–1571), a Florentine sculptor, goldsmith, and pupil of Michelangelo, made an extraordinary button in 1530 for Pope Clement VII, depicting God the Father, surrounded by cherubs.

The button was mounted on gold and decorated with diamonds and other precious stones. It has since disappeared, but the British Museum has a representation of it in a watercolor by F. Bartoli.

Ferrotype (or tintype) buttons are from 1860–1900, and were worn by men going to war, who inserted pictures of their mothers, wives, or sweethearts in them.

MID 19TH-CENTURY
AMERICAN TINTYPE

The earliest type of locket buttons were made in Paris, during the reign of Louis XVI, and contained tiny pornographic scenes.

Among other things,
buttons have
commemorated
famous architectural
sights, such as the
Statue of Liberty
and the Eiffel Tower.

In the late 1930s, celluloid-covered buttons containing pictures of M. G. M. movie stars were made for fans. Stars they celebrated include Loretta Young, Robert Taylor, Errol Flynn, Clark Gable, Tyrone Power, and Myrna Loy.

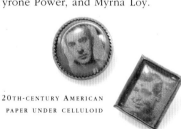

20TH-CENTURY AMERICAN
PAPER UNDER CELLULOID

On a famous hunting trip in Mississippi in 1902, President Teddy Roosevelt refused to shoot a bear cub. The "teddy" bear soon became a decorative motif, adorning boxes, postcards, tea sets, lamps, puzzles, and of course, buttons.

When prohibition was repealed in 1933, Americans went wild for depictions of liquor. Not surprisingly, button designs from the 1930s celebrated cocktail glasses and whiskey bottles. Buttons in the mid-1930s also reflected the growing popularity of the big band sound.

EARLY 20TH-CENTURY
AMERICAN BRASS

Entertainer Carmen Miranda
inspired thousands
of fruit-themed buttons
manufactured in
the 1930s and 1940s.

The glamorization of the Duchess of Windsor's jewels along with fashion designer Coco Chanel's embrace of costume jewelry led to widespread use of rhinestones in designs of the 1930s and 1940s.

Famous designers of buttons include Cartier, Faberge, Tiffany & Co., Liberty & Co., Battersea (English enamels), Porcelain, Minton, Wedgwood, Sevres, Delft, Meissen, and Wemyss.

Common materials buttons are made of include copper, brass, pewter, steel, aluminum, silver, gold, porcelain, enamel, glass, pearl, shell, horn, bone, rubber, vegetable, ivory, wood, cloth, composition, and plastics.

LATE 19TH-CENTURY
ESKIMO-CARVED
FOSSILIZED IVORY

Some of the more unusual materials
buttons are made of include pota-
toes, straw, shark's tooth, chicken
skin, soapstone, cork, nuts, peach
pits, fossilized walrus tusk, lava
stone, and black forest staghorn.

Poison buttons have a sharp stud on the top of them that was attached to a tiny vial, which was hidden under the assassin's garment. The wearer could scratch his victim's skin with the stud simply by brushing by him in a crowded room. The poison from the vial would instantly penetrate the victim's abrasion.

LATE 17TH-CENTURY
AUSTRO-HUNGARIAN
GILDED SILVER,
ENAMELED, AND JEWELED
SMUGGLER'S BUTTON

Smuggler's buttons have hollow, dome-shaped tops that twist off to reveal a space for hiding small but valuable objects, such as diamonds or messages. Some of these twist-apart buttons looked exactly like army issue uniform buttons and were issued to special commando outfits. These contained poison, probably for the soldier's personal use in case of torture.

Garter buttons, which showed flappers' faces, were popular between 1910–1920. Purely decorative, these risqué buttons were worn on the outside of stockings, just below the knees. Each one was covered with cotton or silk and had a painted face on it.

This book has been bound using
handcraft methods, and was Smyth-sewn
to ensure durability.

The dust jacket and interior were designed
by Maria Taffera Lewis

Individual buttons photographed
by Joan Broderick

Still lifes, chapter openers, and end papers
photographed by John Romeo

All buttons shown are from the private collection
of Diana Epstein and Millicent Safro

The text was edited by Mary McGuire

The text was set in
Garamond and Garamond Book